I0838913

LIFE
IN
52
QUOTES

LIFE
IN 52 QUOTES
KIT

LESS IS MORE

Ludwig Mies van der Rohe

INTRODUCTION

We find them everywhere. They are in books, magazine articles, old newspaper clippings and street grafitti. They are overheard on street corners, subway platforms, dive bars and office hallways. They are words that at that moment answer a question we didn't even know we were asking. It's a modern form of bibliomancy.

In a time of information overload, Life In 52 Quotes separates the signal from the noise to bring you a highly curated collection of clever and concise quotes. Here are words that will tell you all you need to know about life, and how to live it.

- Kit

"THIS IS THE WORLD AS IT IS. THIS IS WHERE YOU START."

— SAUL ALINSKY
RULES FOR RADICALS

"WHATEVER YOU DO, KID, ALWAYS SERVE IT WITH A LITTLE DRESSING."

— GEORGE M. COHEN

"IN WALKING THROUGH THE WORLD THERE IS A CHOICE FOR A MAN TO MAKE. HE CAN CHOOSE THE FAIR AND OPEN PATH, THE PATH WHICH SOUND ETHICS, SOUND DEMOCRACY, AND THE COMMON LAW PRESCRIBE, OR CHOOSE THE SECRET WAY BY WHICH HE CAN GET THE BETTER OF HIS FELLOW MAN."

— IDA TARBELL
ALL IN A DAYS WORK: AN AUTOBIOGRAPHY

"IT IS OF NO CONSEQUENCE WHAT OTHERS THINK OF YOU. WHAT MATTERS IS WHAT YOU THINK OF THEM. THAT IS HOW YOU LIVE YOUR LIFE."

— GORE VIDAL

"NOT EVERYTHING THAT IS FACED CAN BE CHANGED, BUT NOTHING CAN BE CHANGED UNTIL IT IS FACED."

— JAMES BALDWIN

"THE MORE YOU STRUGGLE TO LIVE, THE LESS YOU LIVE. GIVE UP THE NOTION THAT YOU MUST BE SURE OF WHAT YOU ARE DOING. INSTEAD, SURRENDER TO WHAT IS REAL WITHIN YOU, FOR THAT ALONE IS SURE.....YOU ARE ABOVE EVERYTHING DISTRESSING."

— SPINOZA

"ONE OF OUR CIVIL LIBERTIES IS TO BE PECULIAR."

— CLAIRE FRASER-LIGGETT
WIRED MAGAZINE

"WHEN YOU CHOOSE YOUR FRIENDS, DON'T BE SHORT-CHANGED BY CHOOSING PERSONALITY OVER CHARACTER."

— W.SOMERSET MAUGHAM

"PLANS ARE ALL RIGHT SOMETIMES, AND SOMETIMES JUST STIRRING THINGS UP IS ALL RIGHT."

— DASHIELL HAMMET

RED HARVEST

"WE WORK IN THE DARK - WE DO WHAT WE CAN - WE GIVE WHAT WE HAVE. OUR DOUBT IS OUR PASSION, AND OUR PASSION IS OUR TASK. THE REST IS THE MADNESS OF ART."

— HENRY JAMES
THE MIDDLE YEARS

"THERE'S A WHOLE CATEGORY OF PEOPLE WHO MISS OUT BY NOT ALLOWING THEMSELVES TO BE WEIRD ENOUGH."

— ALAIN DE BOTTON

"ANY TIME THINGS
APPEAR TO BE
GOING BETTER,
YOU HAVE
OVERLOOKED
SOMETHING."

— SHIRLEY CHISHOLM

"IF YOU HAVE NO CRITICS YOU'LL LIKELY HAVE NO SUCCESS."

— MALCOLM X

"THINK BEFORE YOU SPEAK. READ BEFORE YOU THINK."

— FRAN LEBOWITZ
THE FRAN LEBOWITZ READER

'… THE GAME HAD NEVER BEEN FAIR, THE DICE WERE LOADED. THEY WERE SWINDLERS AND THIEVES OF PENNIES AND DIMES, AND THEY HAD BEEN TRAPPED AND PUT OUT OF THE WAY BY THE SWINDLERS AND THIEVES OF MILLIONS OF DOLLARS."

— UPTON SINCLAIR

THE JUNGLE

"BEFORE YOU DIAGNOSE YOURSELF WITH DEPRESSION OR LOW SELF-ESTEEM, FIRST MAKE SURE THAT YOU ARE NOT, IN FACT, JUST SURROUNDED BY ASSHOLES."

— @DEBIHOPE

"THE SCARIEST
MONSTERS ARE
THE ONES THAT
LURK WITHIN OUR
SOULS..."

— EDGAR ALLAN POE

"NEVER PASS UP A CHANCE TO HAVE SEX OR APPEAR ON TELEVISION."

— GORE VIDAL

"FINISH EVERY DAY AND BE DONE WITH IT. FOR MANNERS AND FOR WISE LIVING IT IS A VICE TO REMEMBER. YOU HAVE DONE WHAT YOU COULD; SOME BLUNDERS AND ABSURDITIES NO DOUBT CREPT IN; FORGET THEM AS SOON AS YOU CAN. TOMORROW IS A NEW DAY; YOU SHALL BEGIN IT WELL AND SERENELY, AND WITH TOO HIGH A SPIRIT TO BE CUMBERED WITH YOUR OLD NONSENSE. THIS DAY FOR ALL THAT IS GOOD AND FAIR. IT IS TOO DEAR, WITH ITS HOPES AND INVITATIONS, TO WASTE A MOMENT ON THE ROTTEN YESTERDAYS."

— RALPH WALDO EMERSON
LETTER TO HIS DAUGHTER, ELLEN

"RESENTMENT IS LIKE DRINKING POISON AND WAITING FOR THE OTHER PERSON TO DIE."

— CARRIE FISHER
WISHFUL DRINKING

"TIME IS THE COIN OF YOUR LIFE. YOU SPEND IT. DO NOT ALLOW OTHERS TO SPEND IT FOR YOU."

— CARL SANDBURG

'...ANY SIGNIFICANT CHANGE IN HUMAN CONSCIOUSNESS CAN BE DISSOLVED IF YOU BREAK IT DOWN INTO ITS INDIVIDUAL PARTS, WHICH ARE BOUND TO SEEM CONTRADICTORY OR MANY-SIDED—YOU CAN DISSOLVE ANYTHING BY DISSOLVING IT. THE ITALIAN RENAISSANCE CAN BE ARGUED OUT OF EXISTENCE AS EASILY AS THE SPANISH INQUISITION.'

— ADAM GOPNIK
THE NEW YORKER

"OURS IS ESSENTIALLY A TRAGIC AGE, SO WE REFUSE TO TAKE IT TRAGICALLY."

— D.H. LAWRENCE
LADY CHATTERLEY'S LOVER

"TIME MOVES IN ONE DIRECTION, MEMORY IN ANOTHER."

— WILLIAM GIBSON
DISTRUST THAT PARTICULAR FLAVOR

"DO NOT LET ME HEAR OF THE WISDOM OF OLD MEN, BUT RATHER OF THEIR FOLLY."

— T.S. ELIOT
FOUR QUARTETS

"SOMETIMES I THINK I'VE FIGURED OUT SOME ORDER IN THE UNIVERSE, BUT THEN I FIND MYSELF IN FLORIDA."

— SUSAN ORLEAN
THE ORCHID THIEF

'THAT WAS THE YEAR, MY TWENTY-EIGHTH, WHEN I WAS DISCOVERING THAT NOT ALL OF THE PROMISES WOULD BE KEPT, THAT SOME THINGS ARE IN FACT IRREVOCABLE AND THAT IT HAD COUNTED AFTER ALL, EVERY EVASION AND EVERY PROCRASTINATION, EVERY MISTAKE, EVERY WORD, ALL OF IT.'

— JOAN DIDION
GOODBYE TO ALL THAT

"ONLY A MEDIOCRE PERSON IS ALWAYS AT HIS BEST. "

— W. SOMERSET MAUGHAM

"A LITTLE
REBELLION NOW
AND THEN IS A
GOOD THING."

— THOMAS JEFFERSON

"OBSTACLES ARE THOSE FRIGHTENING THINGS YOU SEE WHEN YOU TAKE YOU EYES OFF YOUR GOAL."

— HENRY JAMES

"DON'T COMPLAIN ABOUT OUR COFFEE; SOMEDAY YOU MAY BE OLD AND WEAK YOURSELF."

— UPTON SINCLAIR

OIL!

'ARCHITECTURE HAS ALWAYS BEEN THE PHYSICAL INDEX OF HUMAN FAILURE. EVERY GREAT PALACE OR TEMPLE OR FINANCIAL-SERVICES HEADQUARTERS IS A TESTAMENT TO A SOCIETY THAT NEEDED SOMETHING HUGE IN WHICH TO BURY ITS CONTRADICTIONS."

— SAM KRISS
NEW YORK TIMES

"IT IS DIFFICULT TO GET A MAN TO UNDERSTAND SOMETHING, WHEN HIS SALARY DEPENDS ON HIS NOT UNDERSTANDING IT."

— UPTON SINCLAIR

I, CANDIDATE FOR GOVERNOR AND HOW I GOT LICKED

'WE WENT OUR
SEPARATE WAYS,
BUT WITHIN
WALKING
DISTANCE OF ONE
ANOTHER."

— PATTI SMITH
JUST KIDS

"ALMOST NOTHING IMPORTANT THAT EVER HAPPENS TO YOU HAPPENS BECAUSE YOU ENGINEER IT."

— DAVID FOSTER WALLACE
INFINITE JEST

"LEARNING FROM EXPERIENCE IS A FACULTY ALMOST NEVER PRACTICED."

— BARBARA TUCHMAN

THE MARCH OF FOLLY: FROM TROY TO VIETNAM

"I'M ME, AND WHAT THE HELL CAN I DO ABOUT IT!....I, THE SOLEM INVESTIGATOR OF USELESS THINGS."

— ALVARO DE CAMPOS

POEM #481

'THE MOMENT YOU GIVE UP YOUR PRINCIPLES, AND YOUR VALUES, YOU ARE DEAD, YOUR CULTURE IS DEAD, YOUR CIVILIZATION IS DEAD. PERIOD."

— ORIANA FALLACI

'WORK HARD, DO THE BEST YOU CAN, DON'T EVER LOSE FAITH IN YOURSELF AND TAKE NO NOTICE OF WHAT OTHER PEOPLE SAY ABOUT YOU."

— NOËL COWARD

"WE WERE RAISING OUR STANDARD OF LIVING AT THE EXPENSE OF OUR STANDARD OF CHARACTER."

— IDA TARBELL
ALL IN A DAYS WORK: AN AUTOBIOGRAPHY

"WHAT DO YOU THINK OF ME?" "YOU'RE ALL RIGHT," I TOLD HIM, "AND YOU'RE ALL WRONG."

— DASHIELL HAMMET
THE THIN MAN

"EVENTUALLY ALL THINGS ARE KNOWN. AND FEW MATTER."

— GORE VIDAL
BURR, A NOVEL

"DEFEAT SHOULD NOT BE THE SOURCE OF DISCOURAGEMENT, BUT A STIMULUS TO KEEP PLOTTING."

— SHIRLEY CHISHOLM

'WE DIG UP DINOSAURS TO TRY AND FIGURE OUT WHAT HAPPENED TO THEM. PERHAPS SOMEDAY DINOSAURS, IN THE FORM OF CORVIDS, WILL DIG US UP TO FIGURE OUT WHAT HAPPENED TO US."

— JENNIFER ACKERMAN

THE BIRD WAY: A NEW LOOK AT HOW BIRDS TALK, WORK, PLAY, PARENT, AND THINK

"THE PAST IS A
PEBBLE IN MY
SHOE."

— EDGAR ALLAN POE

"YOU CAN'T BECOME NORMAL BY PRETENDING YOU ARE."

— DAVID CARR
THE NIGHT OF THE GUN

'MOST PEOPLE GET A FAIR AMOUNT OF FUN OUT OF THEIR LIVES, BUT ON BALANCE LIFE IS SUFFERING, AND ONLY THE VERY YOUNG OR THE VERY FOOLISH IMAGINE OTHERWISE."

— GEORGE ORWELL

"STUMBLING IS NOT FALLING."

— MALCOLM X

'I DON'T KNOW WHERE I'M GOING, BUT I'M ON MY WAY."

— CARL SANDBURG

"VERY FEW OF US
ARE WHAT WE
SEEM."

— AGATHA CHRISTIE
THE MAN IN THE MIST

'LIFE IS RARELY ABOUT WHAT HAPPENED; IT'S MOSTLY ABOUT WHAT WE THINK HAPPENED."

— CHUCK KLOSTERMAN

SEX, DRUGS, AND COCOA PUFFS: A LOW CULTURE MANIFESTO

"I CHOSE TO SEEK MY FORTUNE. FAILED. LOST ALL. THEN GOT A FORTUNE I HAD NOT EVER LOOKED FOR. LOST IT THOUGH. GOT IT BACK. LOST IT. GOT ANOTHER - THE STORY IS SOMEWHAT REPETITIOUS."

— NEAL STEPHENSON
THE SYSTEM OF THE WORLD

ABOUT THE AUTHOR

it is a reader, writer, listener, and watcher of the human condition.